PAPER

d r e a m s

NANCY GERBER AND ROSEMARY MCGEE
EDITORS

PAPER

d r e a m s

WRITINGS FROM THE

ACAP
WRITE TO HEAL
GROUP

ARSEYA PUBLISHING * NEW JERSEY

Library of Congress Control Number: 2017940874

ISBN: 978-1-935093-09-1

Cover art by Judy Lapides
Back cover photo by Susan Saunders
Cover/text design by Curtis Tow Graphics, New York, NY
Edited by Nancy Gerber & Rosemary McGee
Printed in the U.S. by The Wall Street Group, South Plainfield, NJ

Published by Arseya Publishing
New Vernon, New Jersey
www.arseya.com

FIRST EDITION

"People think dreams aren't
real just because they
aren't made of matter, of particles.
Dreams are real. But they are
made of viewpoints, of images, of
memories and puns and lost hopes.
Writing is flying in dreams."

—NEIL GAIMAN

CONTENTS

F O R E W O R D

DR. PATRICIA BRATT

"I'll do it," grinned Dr. Nancy Gerber when I asked in 2012 if she would run a series of workshops, "Write to Heal," for our institute, the Academy of Clinical and Applied Psychoanalysis (ACAP). An expressive writing experience would provide an important addition to our Trauma and Resilience Studies courses. I knew Nancy as an advanced clinical candidate at ACAP through her generous help organizing some of our events, her participation in my Trauma-Resilience classes, as a published author, and former English professor. Always sensitive and enthusiastic, she brought a welcoming air of collaboration, along with her expertise facilitating writing groups, to our experiment. What a success it is.

In short time Nancy approached me to say she would like to bring in a colleague, another ACAP clinical candidate, Dr. Rosemary McGee, to partner with her in the groups: there was demand for additional sections. Rosemary McGee, DMH, a strong supporter of our Trauma-Resilience classes, also a published writer and a publisher, quickly took up the opportunity. Together, she and Nancy have led and expanded the "Write to Heal" series.

I want to emphasize how important "Write to Heal" is for our community, both professionals and those who come looking for a space where they can sort through life's issues in a relaxed, encouraging environment. As Maya Angelou said, "There is no greater an agony than bearing an untold story within you." Over the years many of the groups' participants have provided testimonials to the lightness of spirit, despite often challenging revelations, and connectedness they experience as part of "Write to Heal."

In *Paper Dreams: Writings from the ACAP Write to Heal Group*, Nancy and Rosemary bring together a compendium of pieces of their own and fellow writing group members. These essays and poems tell a story of life in motion as well as reflection. They touch on transformational moments in relationships and self-awareness with awe and humor. What is more moving than recognizing that the detested beige of your childhood home is now the soothing tone decorating yours and connecting you to emotional beginnings? Or what more delightful than reliving through sharing the memory of your first apartment, the neighborhood, and how completely they marked the launch of a long, life stage?

Some of the pieces in *Paper Dreams* are fraught, some funny. All are acknowledgement of the healing power of writing and sharing. They are a tribute to Nancy Gerber's and Rosemary McGee's willingness to encourage creativity and transformation, to help unravel unconscious agendas, and to demonstrate another way words can make a world of difference.

—PATRICIA HARTE BRATT, PhD
Director, ACAP — BGSP-NJ
Livingston, New Jersey

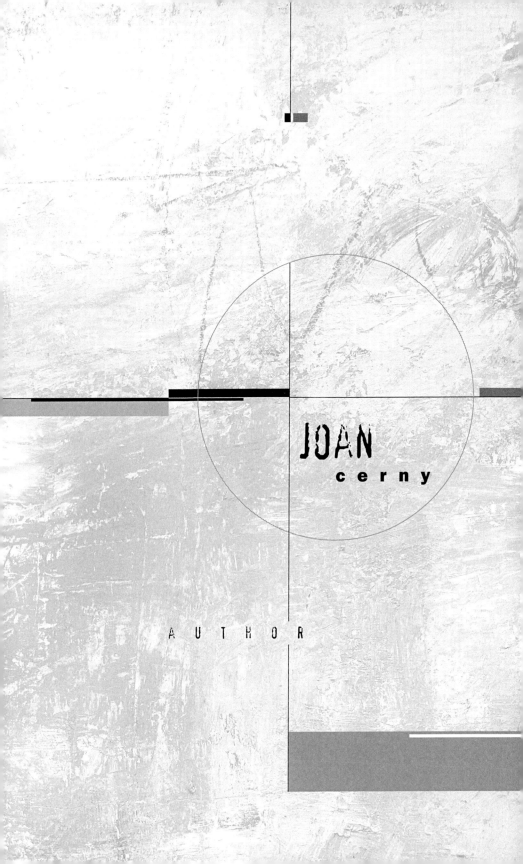

JOAN
cerny

AUTHOR

To My Maternal Grandmother, Who Died Right After She Heard I Was Born

What was it like leaving Frignano, Italy, to come to New York with a husband who felt that he was forced to marry you because you were pregnant with Uncle Jimmy?

What was it like living in the dark tenements of Hester and Mulberry streets after sunny, warm Frignano? Were you cold all winter?

Did it hurt that Americans called Italians "wops"? Did you know that? Was it too much caring for the children by yourself? You must have been devastated after losing your young baby. Was that before or after my mom Philomena was born?

Did your husband Frank hit you because he had been angry since you took him to court in Italy to force a marriage? Was he afraid of you because you threatened him with a gun back then?

Did you really do that?

Did you regret forcing him to marry you? Did you love him or hate him or both?

Did you have a nervous breakdown? Were you crazy? Did you threaten to throw your baby out the window? Did a neighbor hear this and call the authorities who carted you away to a hospital?

Did the doctors tell you that you needed a break and should return to Italy for a while? Did they tell you that your family would be joining you? Did you feel tricked? How could you get on that boat alone?

Who did you live with when you returned to Italy? Did you miss your daughter Philomena? Is that why you sent her jewelry over the years?

What was it like leaving your four-year-old daughter, two-year-old son, older son and husband behind? How come you stayed away for so long? Were your immigration papers really burned in a fire?

Were you only able to return when Uncle Jimmy became of age and could bring you back with him?

Why did you take the jewelry you had sent to my mother and mail it back to a young girl you had befriended during your absence? How could you be so cruel?

Was it a blessing or a curse that you returned when your daughter was fourteen years old? Did your family feel like strangers to you?

Why didn't you teach your daughter how to cook? Did you ever learn to speak English?

Did you hate your husband and children because they had become Presbyterians?

My Four-Year-Old Mother

The four year old with bright eyes, small pert nose and dark hair was confused. Where was her mother? She shuddered when men in a white truck put Mom on a stretcher and took her away. Why couldn't she go along too? Would Mom be back soon? Was this because she had yelled at her younger brother Tony? Mom had been angry and threatened to throw someone out the window but she did not mean it. A neighbor heard her say this and called the authorities who took her to the hospital. Who would take care of her? The girl guessed that it was her fault. Her father had a sad, angry look on his face. He had come home from his tailor shop and was just sitting and staring. Her older brother yelled that it was his father's fault.

■ ▦ | |

MY GRANDFATHER

here is my wife?

How will I care for my children?

The shop must stay open so that we can eat!

Our Lady of Pompeii won't help us.

Anyway, I have hated the Catholic Church since I lost hearing in my right ear after a beating from a nun.

I have heard that they are welcoming at The Broome Street Tabernacle and have kind women missionaries.

Maybe these Presbyterians can help.

ME, THE GRANDDAUGHTER

hree years before she died my mother told me that she had been a foster child for part of her childhood. That explained why she had trouble performing some normal household tasks: no one had taught her how to cook or do the wash. The story is vague but I believe that the kids went back and forth between their father's house and foster care. As they grew older they became very involved with the church and the devoted parish workers. I remember my mother and Uncle Tony speaking of them with great affection.

My mom very rarely spoke about her mother and never mentioned where she was buried. After living in Queens for ten years I discovered that my grandmother was buried four blocks from my house in St. John's Cemetery.

My ninety-three-year-old godmother Agnes says that I look like my maternal grandmother. I strain to see the resemblance but I've only seen a picture of her looking out from an upper window in Little Italy when she was elderly. I am sure that my resemblance to her mother contributed to my mother's expressions of love and dramatic anger towards me as I grew older. I, the daughter, took her mother's place.

I did not wish for this as a child but would have loved to know this maternal grandmother who died the same week I was born. Or maybe I was better off not knowing her... . My mother was not told of the death until after the funeral! A bizarre experience: reminiscent of the way her mother disappeared when she was four years old.

Years later, before I knew that Mom had been in foster care, I found myself working as an "Adoption Home Finder" for Little Flower Children's Services in Brooklyn Heights, New York. It was the best job I have ever had.

WISH I COULD SEE HER NOW: A GENTLER BRONX TALE

Christine and I were playing dress-up wearing my mom's old hats. I had her ostrich plume fuzzy wedding hat perched on my head. We were carrying slim rectangular pocketbooks with short straps and a gold buckle on top center. We checked ourselves in the mirror and took off, walking down our block.

First we ran into crazy Joe who didn't say anything nasty for a change (he probably suffered from schizophrenia). Hannah, the cranky old lady on the first floor, was looking out the window again. She liked to yell at us kids if we were too noisy. If we went too close to her window we were hit by a strong rancid smell of god knows what. As we neared the end of the block we both stiffened because we spied the serious Sister Scholastica, Christine's teacher, approaching in the opposite direction. We both greeted her and almost genuflected! I was afraid of her even though I didn't go to Catholic School.

Christine was about six months younger than me, the eldest of four girls living two floors above my family's apartment. She was easygoing with dimples and a ready smile. Her mom had at least two miscarriages before she was born and tended to overfeed her girls in an effort to keep them alive. I remember her bringing bags of candy on excursions. It was so easy to run a few floors up and find someone to play with.

Sometimes we were outside playing Red Light Green Light or Red Rover on the sidewalk. We walked or rode our bikes to Bronx Park, a block away, and went to the playground (where I told her the facts of life over a Nok-Hockey game one day). Next to the playground was "the circle." This was a horseshoe slate half circle that was a short wall. Part of our routine was balancing atop the circle.

Right next to the circle was a short berry tree which was easy to climb. We viewed this tree as our own personal property and looked askance at any interlopers invading our space. We waited every summer for the delicious dark purple berries. Was it a mulberry tree? I wonder if that tree is still there. On the way to the park was a pussy willow bush that seemed like a miracle. Cat's fur on a bush!

Other summer fun was sitting in the long cool alleyway next to my building reading. I remember crying to *Little Women*, *Jo's Boys* and *Uncle Tom's Cabin*. The library was a few blocks away and it was safe back then for children to walk up the hill to the Lowerre Place branch.

Christine's large family moved to a more comfortable one family house—still in the Bronx but much too far to walk to. We still saw one another as teenagers and college students but gradually lost touch.

Years passed. My sister Carol ran into Christine's Aunt Helen in a bank. She said that Christine was quite ill with cancer. I wrote her a letter remembering our childhoods together and the berry tree. She was thrilled to hear from me and could not believe that I remembered climbing that tree with her. We had a reunion and shared a great time. I met her husband and two sons. She told stories about her teaching career.

Christine died of cancer a few months later. I was getting dressed to go to her funeral when I got a call from my sister. Carol said that Mom had a massive stroke and I needed to get to the hospital immediately. My mother died at two o'clock the next morning. I never made it to Christine's funeral.

I feel jealous of other people who still have their friends from grade school.

ANOTHER LIFE

I have never felt more at home anywhere before or since.

The cute Hungarian "super" was standing in front of 215 West 75th Street smoking a cigarette. That is how I ended up living at 75th & Broadway across from the Beekman Theater and Fairway Market. My friend Marcia and I were 27 years old with long hair. I spoke with the super and told him I was part Hungarian.

My studio apartment had a separate kitchen and dressing room. The dressing room had a huge mirror to twirl around in front of, built-in drawers and just enough room for a bed. The noisiness of the city comforted me. I loved the clanging fire engines, honking taxis and people of every size, shape and color. I was nurtured by the crowds. I was curious about the notorious Plato's Retreat in the Ansonia Hotel. Upon visiting I found many middle-aged men with big stomachs looking for some action. It was a time of free love. The AIDS epidemic had not yet begun.

The food and restaurant revolution hit New York City. America's palate was finally exploding. Julia Child had introduced better quality food and jello molds were becoming a thing of the past. The riotous colors of the produce at Fairway were an art form. The jammed store overflowed with cheeses, bread, pasta, olive oil, vinegars and meats of every kind. Shopping at Zabar's and Fairway became a recreational activity. Fairway even bought the mocha cheesecakes that I produced in my tiny oven across the street. It was a time of eating many calories and not gaining weight.

There were novel new ethnic restaurants on every avenue and side street. Teachers Restaurant near Zabar's made fabulous Chicken Gai Yang—introducing me to Thai food. The nearby Silver Palate gourmet food shop was started by two young women: Julie Rosso and Sheila Lukins, who became famous and produced several best-selling cookbooks. These heady food adventures contributed to my later decision to go to cooking school (along with my father's good cooking and enthusiasm).

I met my husband-to-be the day after I signed the lease to my apartment. We explored the Upper West Side together. He was able to ride his bicycle from my apartment to work on Pine Street in lower Manhattan during a transit strike.

When I no longer lived there I felt that I had left a large part of my best self behind.

EILEEN
erbeck

AUTHOR

FAERIE TALES

I lived in a world of faeries and angels.

My reality was fantasy.

The harsh reality of my daily life was...less than cheery.

But my fantasy (or what I made my reality) world was enchanting!

Tinker Bell, flying dreams, angels who kept me safe

Were so much more real than the greyness around me.

"Our Silly Eileen" wove a life that saved her...for awhile.

After a time, these words chased away the faeries.

I missed them.

They were always there at the periphery, though.

Carried away on the occasional magic carpet ride by a song
or a piece of art

I survived.

The magic is more in my life now.

I sing, I write, I make art.

I feed my soul.

Welcome back!

Closing the Drapes

If you leave the drapes open

You leave yourself vulnerable to all things.

*Everyone, every*thing can see you.

Down into your soul they see your fears — who you are.

Why not just close them?

Safe from all the bad things that won't be, *can't* be talked about.

Sssh...hide it all.

Stuff it in the sofa — no one will see.

Keep the drapes closed tight.

In your cocoon.

Safe and warm and dark.

No one can see you now.

No wounds, no fears, no vulnerabilities.

You're safe.

Too safe?

What would sneak in if I opened the drapes?

A whiff of lavender from beyond the French doors?

The crickets and frogs with their nighttime sonatas

Sung just for me?

The far-off train whistle bringing me back.

Why was that still so reassuring?

Did it lull me to sleep

Bringing the promise of far-off places, secure in a sleeping car

With drapes pulled tightly shut?

Clickety clack clickety clack

Close the drapes, open the drapes

Close them, open them.

Try it both ways, try it both ways.

Woo-ooh woo-ooh.

GOING

It's hard not to go there — the empty place that's still filled with longing.

I can't bear to go there unless I'm feeling strong.

That's wrong...when I'm strong I don't need to go there.

When I'm empty and can't find the missing pieces, I go there

Searching endlessly...

Usually coming back before I'm too lost in my worn-out sorrow.

Happy and pretty — not second nature to me.

I practice going there, though...

Hoping to feel more at home each time.

'Til the sun goes behind a cloud.

'Til the pit of my stomach calls me back.

PROMISES TO COME

In the attic of my mind

Everything gathers dust that I've stored away...

Not wanting to deal with it.

Not organized in carefully labeled boxes

But helter skelter in a mix of emotions.

Boxes of bric-a-brac left

Perhaps for the next generation to deal with.

Passing on not only unresolved conflicts

But the musty cabinets of memories long forgotten.

Until a breath of fresh air blows through to clear things out.

Just like the aftereffects of a cathartic session

Or a long needed cry.

Just like it feels when you throw open the window of a dusty attic

And let in the air and sunshine

And deal with your long-held possessions

And promises to come.

BLOWING

The old years blow back

As an icy wind

Or a spring breeze caressing my face.

A new infatuation stirs the soft wind into a lover's whisper.

How I long for it.

Can't wait for it.

Close my eyes and surrender.

The icy wind of despair, disappointment, betrayal.

No wonder I despise the winter.

It hurts. It stings.

Layers of sadness.

The warmth, the sea.

Few clothes, deep breaths, langorous movements.

Warrior poses.

I am a warrior.

Yes, I can breathe.

The years blow back and once more, I'm there.

NANCY
gerber

AUTHOR

BEIGE

eige. Everything in my mother's house was beige. Accented with tones of off-white, cream, or ivory. The living room walls were beige, the sofa was beige, the upholstery on the chairs and the piano bench was—you guessed it—beige. My mother was known as the Queen of Beige.

I grew up hating the color beige. It was the hue of washed-out mud, the opposite of colorful. It lacked depth and sparkle. It was a whitewashing of emotion, rebellion, spontaneity—all the things I wanted in my life. When I was a teenager, I believed everything my mother feared and tried to hide was hidden beneath many layers of beige.

In my new house, where I've lived for nearly two years, everything is—I'm embarrassed to tell you—beige. Maybe not exactly beige, because I've been working with a decorator, who has a keen eye for the new and elegant, but, nonetheless, soft, muted, earthy tones of taupe. There's some sparkle, too, crystal and mirrored glass, but the overall look is a creamy kind of beige.

Beige is my favorite color.

Mean Girls I Have Known

I went to sleep-away camp with one of the meanest girls alive, Marcy Feinberg.

She hated me, I don't know why. I was a shy goody-two-shoes who liked the counselors better than my fellow campers. I think she saw in me someone she could victimize. Now, with the perspective of many years, I realize she was probably bullied at home or perhaps abused.

After swimming lessons at the lake, when no one else was around, she would sidle up to me and say nasty things: mock my frizzy hair and glasses, snicker at my pudgy body. I would write letters home complaining about her but my parents weren't particularly sympathetic. Among many post-Holocaust Jews at the time, the feeling was it was better to be the bully than the victim.

In my final year at Cedar Lake I was placed in the same bunk as my tormentor. I walked into the cabin and saw her sitting there, cross-legged on her cot. When she saw me, her eyes lit up. Let the games begin! She began an interrogation, as though I were on trial: did I smoke? Did I have a boyfriend and how far had I gone? Would I help torture the counselors?

I knew I could not live in the same place as she did, so I went to the division head and asked to be switched. I was assigned to a new bunk with nice girls, some who became my friends that summer. I kissed a boy for the first time after he walked me home from a dance. I've never given myself credit for standing up for what I needed.

Five years later my mother told me Marcy Feinberg sat inside a closed garage in her mother's car with the windows shut tight and the engine idling. At the age of 17, she was dead. I knew I should have felt sorry for her, but at the time I didn't.

DISHES I COVETED

My grandmother's blue and white willow dishes sat on the shelves of her dining room hutch. I coveted this set, its Orientalist images of pagodas and cherry trees evoking foreign lands. My grandmother was foreign born but so different from the blue and white dishes. They were fragile and easily chipped whereas my grandmother was sturdy. She had survived life in a new land; she was unbreakable. I was just a child; what did I know?

My grandmother suffered from all kinds of demons, anxieties and fears that haunted her. When she was ten she survived a pogrom in Ekaterinaslav in the Ukraine. One hundred Jews were slaughtered, ten of them children. She was a Jewish child. She must have been in terror for her life.

My grandmother never learned to read or write. To her dying day she could only sign her name with an X. People used to ask me why she never learned. My response was: when was she supposed to do that? Between raising three children in a country where she barely spoke the language and working side by side with my grandfather, a tailor, while trying to survive the Great Depression, when was there time? And who was there to tell her she should learn?

I wanted those blue and white dishes after my grandmother died but they went to my nasty Aunt Florence. When my grandmother's linens and silvers were laid out on the dining room table I did manage to take three plates from my aunt without her knowing. Or maybe my mother had already insisted that some of that set belonged to me.

BROKEN

(AFTER SHARON OLDS)

Some things cannot be fixed.

A cracked egg, a porcelain plate

in shards on the floor.

I want to repair things that cannot be mended.

Days wrenched by depression.

My father's leg, withered from stroke.

Six years in a wheelchair

Each day dragging an anger so great

it tore clouds from the sky.

A storm that rent my parents' marriage.

I want to mend the space between me

and my son, thousands of miles,

days cut off from mine.

EMILY DICKINSON'S HANDS

Pale as alabaster, delicate yet strong.

If not, how was there so much force

In her words. "After great pain,

A formal feeling comes." Those long em dashes,

Exclamation points! Her fingers dashing

Across the page, a herd of wild horses.

In photographs her face unsmiling,

Withdrawn from the world. And yet

Her words, etched in marble.

She must have had strong hands.

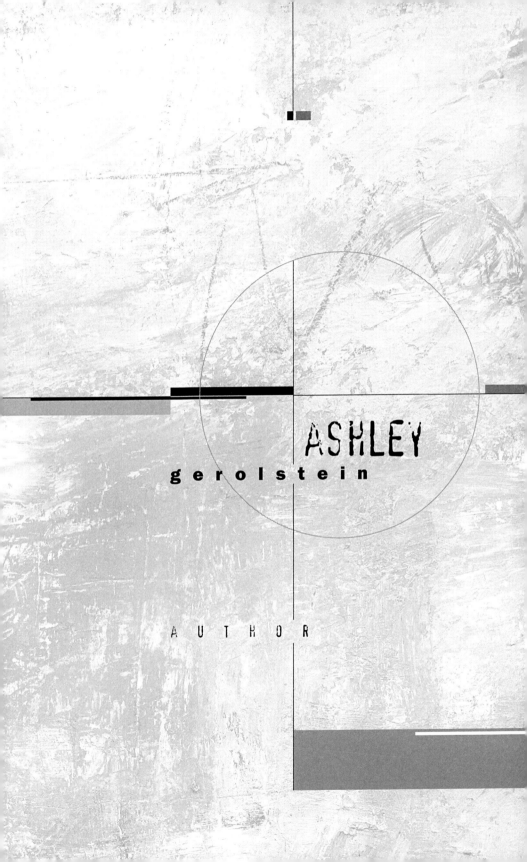

ASHLEY

gerolstein

AUTHOR

It All Started...

It all started when I walked through the door. Grandma was sitting in her wheelchair. The curtain was pulled closed behind her. I knew what to expect but at the same time I didn't. I kissed Grams on her cheek and tried to figure out what to say. What do you say to a woman whose partner for 65 years passed away somewhat unexpectedly? What do you say to her? I gave her a great big hug—careful as she was a bag of bones. Kissed my aunt on the cheek as we both sobbed uncontrollably. My first major loss in my adult life. I visibly remember my mother shaking out of control, makeup smearing down her face. Comforting her, we slowly began to disperse Grandpa K's items. First what to do with the pillow he crafted by hand of his first and only dog Lovey. Who keeps it? I look slowly at the hospital bed—that once had a life in it. A life of wisdom and humor. A life that taught me cat's cradle. A life that introduced me to franks and mac 'n' cheese. A life that made 12 pointed origami stars, which now decorate my home. A life that could solve math problems in minutes. A life that literally belonged to my second father. Now, just an empty plastic covered blue mattress. I grab my mom to stifle my tears. I must be strong for them. I must. Over her shoulder, I see their wedding picture, my grandpa's Navy picture, and photos of the family when we were close. I close my eyes to try to escape. He's in a better place I remind myself. He's my guardian angel.

My Grandparents' Car

It was a boat. It wasn't a car. Ridiculously large. Waiting for me out front of school every day with the captain being my grandpa and the co-captain being my grandma. The boat was older than me. Two doors that weighed like a ton of bricks. Far too heavy as the captains became more and more frail. Exactly at 3 pm, my grandma would stand outside the 1980 giant, waiting for me. I'd see her wave. It became embarrassing as I got older to see this boat waiting for me, a boat that was inherited from the captain's brother. But I loved them dearly, and sucked it up Monday, Wednesday, and Friday, kissing my grandma on the cheek, pushing the passenger seat forward to slide into the back. More like maneuver my way into the back seat. Always tons of garbage back there—empty bottles, random pieces of paper, maps to all over the country, curtain rods, tissue boxes. I had to move stuff around just to sit on the seat, placing my backpack on top of the pile that I call junk. I look out the small side window as the co-captain climbs in and pulls the door shut. I sigh as I hear the captain say hi as he puts the directional on as he slowly eases out into traffic.

CODE GREYISH

A big, tough guy. A big fighter. A guy I watched tackle another patient to the floor, blood spewing everywhere. A guy who has cursed at me on multiple occasions. He now sits in front of me in coping skills group. The hood over his head as he looks at the floor. When I asked what should be discussed today, he raises his hand saying he doesn't need discussion, but more support. He tells me he just found out he won't be leaving until mid-January, requiring him to stay through the whole holiday season. Although he's a frequent patient, which he admits, he has never spent the holidays in the hospital. He goes on to tell the group how he doesn't know what freedom is. How he may have only been at the county a few times, but that doesn't include his time at other hospitals and jails. A man who at one time I was physically frightened of is now a man I just want to hold. No love. No freedom.

Later, a doctor approaches me about another patient who's selectively mute, asking me to get him out on community outings. When I ask about finances as I always do, the doctor says he has nothing. No money. No savings. And his brother is his only family, who as of lately has disowned him. He's alone in the world. No family.

I sit in the hallway and watch as patients get discharged. It's bittersweet because although I am happy to see them go, I worry that they will return because of how the system works. Then I see them leaving with two ShopRite bags filled with all their belongings. That's all they own, and I am pretty certain that half was acquired while they were at the hospital. They have the biggest smiles on their faces— even though they have no savings, two bags of clothing, no family. They are being discharged to a group home, where every day will probably be a battle for them. A battle of survival in every sense of the word.

No love. No freedom. No money. No family. But survival…

A TREE'S IMPRINT

can remember the day as if it was yesterday. I still can see the blood streaming from my dad's face at times. I'm very thankful he's alive. I can still hear him yelling at me to not get out of the car. "What are you doing? Where are you going?" Me yelling at him saying we need to get help. I can still remember getting out of the car, doubled over in pain trying to scream for help hoping someone would hear me. Three blocks too far for my mom to hear. I turn around and look at the car, which no longer looked like a car. It looked like a piece of metal nearly cut in two pieces with a tree smack dab in the middle. I can still remember my dad emerging from the wreck, chin completely split open, glass all over his hair. I can still remember a neighbor (a parent of a classmate) running out with a warm blanket encouraging me to sit on the corner. I can still remember her asking me where I exactly lived because she knew I was from the area. I can still remember seeing my mom come running up the street 15 minutes later screaming "Kenny, Ashley. My life. Don't let anything happen to them." I can hear the engines in the distance and the alarms sounding from the local fire departments. I can still remember the police asking me what happened. Was my dad wearing his seat belt? I can still remember the medics telling my mom they were going to take us to LIJ. I can still remember the medics telling me I needed to go on the stretcher even though I was adamant that I was fine. But what can't I remember? I can't remember what caused us to drive into the tree. I can't remember what happened between the stop sign and that tree. The tree, that to this day, continues to hold the imprint of my father's car.

TICK TOCK

Silence
Think too much
Think too little
Tick Tock
Beads of sweat forming
On the brow
Tick tock
Awaiting an answer
Laughter from another
A ping on a cell phone
Tick Tock
Examining one's own self
The rights
The wrongs
Tick Tock
Heart begins to race
The anxiety forms
Tick tock
Relax yourself
Deep breaths
If it's meant to be
Tick Tock
Meant to be
You'll know
Resist the urge
Tick tock
Silence

CHARLENE

mason-reese

AUTHOR

A WORLD HAS OPENED

My writing is becoming meaningful and inspiring to me. I don't write at home, but when I come to the Writing Workshop and start writing, I realize how much I miss doing it, I wonder why I don't write more frequently. The writing awakens something inside of me. Borrowing from C.E. (a member of the writing group), which I may do frequently in this piece, because what she said seemed to be coming from my heart and mind. When she said there is so much in her head, I felt that, I seem to have lots in my head that wants to get out, in the written form. I don't stop and take the time to put thoughts on paper or on screen, but I know that my innards or my soul wants to express itself.

I now want to write as much as I want to read. Reading is essential to me, if someone were to tell me I could never read another book, I would feel they were imposing a death sentence on me. I can feel the writing becoming that essential. There are so many books and not nearly enough time to read them all. I am now recognizing that there are so many subjects that I could write about to express myself. Everything from items in the news, such as the six- or eight-year-old boy suspended for kissing the girl on her hand (sexual harassment) to looking at the snow on the ground, the bare trees, which look beautiful, but do not make me like the cold weather any better.

Yeah, writing is life giving—I am glad it found me.

RED DRESS

The first time I wore a dressy red dress it was a hand-me-down. It was given to me by the lady who employed my mother. I wore the dress the day she and her husband came to dinner; now it seems odd that they would be dining at the home of the woman who cleaned their house, it seemed normal at the time. She told me how good I looked in the red dress. I remember thinking I did not look fat. It was a slim fitting dress and I felt I looked beautiful. I don't remember if red was my favorite color before that day, but it was my chosen one from the palette wheel from then on. There was a time when a woman wearing a red dress was considered a "loose woman" of questionable morals—today, a woman wearing red is considered making a power statement. Today I keep numerous red outfits in my closets, short dresses, pant suits, skirt suits, maxi dresses, dressy dresses, you name the outfit, I probably have it in one of the closets.

The most memorable red dress was worn when I retired. It was my DAY—I had arrived. I floated into the ballroom on the arms of my son in my fabulous red dress and floated throughout the evening. No one had to tell me I was beautiful, I knew I was. My niece had done my make-up impeccably and my hair was arranged by the master. It was all about me; the last time I felt this way was my wedding day, every woman should experience this feeling once in her life, here I was experiencing it twice. I am reliving it as I put it down on paper. As I said, I floated through the evening surrounded by personal and professional people who played a significant role in my life. I had on my red dress, I was saying, SEE ME !!!

PEARLIE MAE

I was a blessed child. I not only had a maternal and paternal grandmother, but I had a paternal great grandmother. All lived within walking distance and were very much involved in my life. We all went to the same church. Out of the three, it was definite I had a favorite, maybe because, nah, I won't try to rationalize it, she was my favorite always—Gramma Johnson, my mother's mother. When I got older I would mess with her by calling her Pearlie Mae. I can still feel, see myself entering her building, walking up the four steps, going down the long hall—yelling as I take each step—"Pearlie Mae! Pearlie Mae! I'm coming." As a little girl, it was, "Gramma, Gramma, Gramma, here I am," running as I would hear her say through the open door, way back from the kitchen, "Come on Charlene, I am waiting for you." I knew she was walking toward the door. I knew she had the black hair net on her head, the print apron tied around her waist (not a nice new apron, mind you, because all the new aprons we bought her for gifts were in boxes in her bottom drawer, neatly kept, never used). Gramma Johnson was the most important person in my life (sorry Mom, sorry husband), until the birth of my son, whom she met and spent several years taking care of.

GONE

My brother/my twin. My first cousin—I looked up the date—I don't remember the exact date, but you died, the first week of June as I drove down H-1 in Hawaii. Penny called, asking, no, not asking, screaming, where was I, she was also yelling that he was gone, I was saying who was gone? She gave you CPR—we tried to contact 911, learned emergency calls do not transfer through states, you have to call directly to the appropriate municipality.

June, July, August, September, October, November and December and I am still reeling. Initially my motto, my mantra was I could not be sadder than the widow, Penny. Penny and I handled that well, we asked each other how we were doing, but avoided probing too deeply.

You were three months younger than me. After your death what immediately came to my mind and has not left it is I don't know how to negotiate this world without you. Even when not seeing you, I knew you were somewhere in the natural universe. When you were going through life's challenges, I never doubted that you would come

I

through. I also thought that you went into never-never land so I didn't have to, you could, would not allow me to.

The first time I thought I was getting married, you had to take the ride all the way down to West Virginia, as the family took me back to school to meet the guy. No one else knew I was serious about the "hillbilly," as you called him. I didn't marry him, but the first time I brought the one around to whom I would say " I do," when he walked in the door the family thought it was you.

A lifetime of memories, your lifetime, but will last my lifetime. I think of two that are so precious. Giving me our grandmother, telling me a conversation you and she had when you were young. Where she acknowledged me as the oldest and told you how much she loved me.

The other was when I questioned how my parents managed to get together. Your response still brings tears: "Char, if they had not gotten together we would not have had you."

I am missing you—I know about the grief process, but getting in the car, driving and not talking to you, old man. The sun does not shine the same way.

THE ME I LIKE

"Like a handkerchief waving goodbye"

    I am waving goodbye to not liking me

To not accepting me

To looking for faults in me

I am now looking at the woman I am

I am celebrating her

I like this lady, without a "but . . ." added

I can look at her and see she is compassionate,

as well as passionate

She is loving, giving, she enjoys being with people.

She loves to laugh, she loves life —

Big Life!!

She wants to explore

■ ▥ ▏

She wants to meet new people, do new things

DISCOVERY—that would be her word for now

Discovering more about herself—finding out what other talents

      may lie below the surface, in addition to the writing.

Discovering the depths of the writing.

What else the writing can reveal about her

What the writing can heal within her, that can enable her to live

      this phase of her life to the fullest

Without the dark clouds trying to get in

She knows there is so much for her to do

Not just for herself

But for and with others

The present and the future are so open to her.

ROSEMARY
mcgee

AUTHOR

IN THE ATTIC

No attic in my contemporary home
No crawl space
No hiding place for old trunks
Full with dress up clothes
Old wedding gowns
Secret letters from past loves
Brooklyn Dodger game programs.

Childhood in Michigan
All houses had attics
Small dormer windows
Looking out on neighbors far below.
Ours a playroom with dolls and toys
We'd escape from kitchen brooms
Vacuums and Mother's big band albums
Broadway show tunes of plays
She had never seen that
Conjured dreams
Sounds of music in the Alps,
Washing that man right out of her head
Trouble in River City.

My sister and I played house
Fisher Price oven baked our cakes
Served on little girl china tea set
We drank with pinkies raised.

In my mind's eye it looks idyllic
Then the stronger memory takes over.
Uncle Don, my favorite
Staggered up to see us
Bailed out of the drunk tank again
Taken in by his sister.
Should have been at a detox center,
Maybe they didn't exist in 1957.

What did we know
About alcohol and its effects?
He just seemed a bit shaky
And weak to us.
We invited him to sit
Share our tea and crumpets.

One minute he was fine, the next
All our toys were splattered with blood.
We were screaming!
Thought he was dying.
Vomiting, retching
Crazed on the floor.

He recovered and recovered
Lived with us again and again.
The attic though lost its magic
Horror remained too real
Bloodstained pink-flowered wallpaper
Never replaced.

INDEPENDENCE

I took my friend to the salon for a haircut
Wheelchair bound, two broken ankles.
Recently out of a cast and free to put weight
She could now propel herself with her feet
As well as her arms, rolling the wheels.
I was happy to see her back in the driver's seat
So to speak, eager to take over, less dependent.

I was reminded that my mother did that
Used her feet while in the wheelchair.
I was with her at the assisted living facility
Taking her to eat in the dining room.
As I pushed her wheelchair along, she would
Periodically put her feet down, stalling the chair
Causing me to stumble.

First time, I said, "Ma, don't do that,
It makes me stumble." I saw an empty seat
Began steering the chair in that direction.
Mom had other ideas and dragged her feet again.
This time, I yelled at her, "Ma, for heavens sake,
Stop it!" Everyone around looked up
To see the abusive daughter shouting

At her feeble mother. Ashamed and angry,
I stopped and said to her, "God damn it Ma,
I'm trying to help you."
"I want to go over there, with Sue," she said.
Maybe I should have asked her
Where she wanted to sit.

Maybe she was being obstinate.
Maybe she just wanted to control one small thing
Since her life had become so dependent
Upon others.

I went there every evening after work
Not wanting her to be alone, feel alone.
I was kind to her. Talked with her.
Loved her.
The only time others saw us together
I was yelling at her, ugly,
My frustration spewing forth unchecked.
Was I loving or hateful?
I'm still not sure.

WELCOME HOME

I open the door
   Just before her knuckles
Rap the wood
Knowing her so well, always
Anticipating her thoughts
Her next move.

Standing there
I step across the threshold
Embrace her
Hold her close,
As she could have done
When I was a child.

Striving to get away from her
Get her out of my psyche
Out from under my skin
Had been a lifelong pursuit.
When she stood at my doorstep
After Dad died, I wasn't ready
To welcome her, although
She lived in my home for two years.

Not willing to forgive or confront
I waited until after
Her death
To tell my truth
To say what had to be said,
Spewing anger and sadness
For her failings,
Misgivings of my childhood.

Now with her in my arms
I see her anew.
I feel her fear and pain
Abuse from her father.
I feel her confusion and grief
When forced to give up
Her first-born son.
I feel her resignment
Marrying Dad.

And I feel her strength.
I know now
She did the best she could
She gave me all she was able to give.
Finally,
I thank her.

VIRGINIA AND POSEIDON

I'm so weary of this life
   Out of characters to help me
Express my pain
I'm left with myself
Unwilling to plunge those depths
Again.

"Yes, my dear (Poseidon, in a whisper
Like a soft breeze through the trees)
Life should be simple
A stroll on the beach
Toes in the sand along the lake.
Look, there's a stone, and another
Perfect for your pockets."

Cool and smooth in my hands
One white, one black
Yin and yang, push and pull, I feel
They're heavy but
I'll keep them.

"Come through the thickets to water's edge
Hear the gentle slapping
See tiny whitecaps break against the shore.
No need to remove your shoes
Step nearer, let the water
Tickle your ankles."

(In her mother's voice
Poseidon beckons her)
"Keep walking to me
Take my hands, Virginia.
Let me hold you
Closer and closer.
There, there
I will make it ok."

So refreshing, wet on my skin.
Universal embrace
Mother calling me home.

AH, PARIS

There is something about Paris
    Maybe it's the lore
Artists, writers producing masterpieces.

Maybe it's L'Amour
Lovers on the Seine
Making wishes
Staring into each other's eyes
Over espresso at a sidewalk café.

It could be the museums
Rodin's garden of sculpture
Mona Lisa's home in the Louvre.
I saw a photo of the Eiffel Tower recently
Being hit by lightening that looked
Grander than the real thing,
But the real thing is grand indeed.

Perhaps it's the bread
Popping into a patisserie or boulangerie
Buying a fresh baguette or brioche
Munching it as I walk down the street.

Smelling the aroma of fresh bread baking.
There is something about Paris.

It's the bread!
Yes, it's the bread!

EDNA

rudolph

AUTHOR

LENOX HILL

Funny I just read a poem about how another mother threatened to abandon her children and go to Bellevue. It reminded me of how my mother threatened the same way. But who at the young age of six could fathom such an event taking place. It did happen, but instead of Bellevue, it was Lenox Hill Hospital.

It was sad that my parents were prone to keep ongoing matters as secrets from their children. But the worst part was that such a threat became real and Mommy did not return home for a week. What did we do to her? What did we say to her? How could we be threatened like this? Who was going to care for us?

The guilt and shame I experienced was pure torture. We never felt so abandoned. My sister was three and I was six and we had no understanding about why this woman would take her suitcase and walk to the elevated subway. We could look out the window and see her on the platform waiting for the train. And then the train came and she was gone.

Daddy was no help. He seemed to have little understanding too. He had yelled at us the night before about why my sister and I were picking on each other. As young as she was, she was a tease, especially about my hair. Hers was lovely and thick and curly and mine was thin and straight. This was a button pusher for me and I would yell to leave me alone. The noise level was horrendous and that would aggravate my mother. And this time, she left.

ROBIN
shimel

AUTHOR

THE APARTMENT

My first apartment, 77 Barrow Street at the corner of Commerce. The owners of the Blue Mill Tavern, a mainstay of the neighborhood, offered rental preference to its employees in an unrenovated brownstone next door. Buses filled with international tourists, eyes glued to the windows, wander down the narrow curving streets for a glimpse of the famous Greenwich Village in New York City. It is 1977.

Through a friend who works as a bartender there and lives next door, I gain entrance and the opportunity to reside in what, to me, is the best block in town. Climbing the four steep, narrow flights I open the door to a railroad flat, three rooms one in back of the other. The kitchen first with a large, claw foot bathtub squeezed between an oversized sink and an undersized refrigerator. A white painted metal counter sits atop the tub. It can be hooked up to the wall for bathing. A disturbing image flashes through my mind of taking a bath while washing dishes. I move on to imagine space for a cafe size table and two small chairs. The stove range is as wide as a small filing cabinet but it works.

The bathroom, a single toilet in the outside hallway. For privacy, a hook and eye inside. I will have to purchase a more substantial lock to prevent outsiders. Not that a stranger would bother to climb four flights to pick "my" lock. Next question, a key or combination for the bathroom door. Concern builds. I might forget the combination in the middle of the night. Then I realize it could be worse to lose a key.

The "living room" is a long narrow windowless space. It might serve well as a passageway in a finer dwelling. A small couch from my childhood home, a possible fit. Walls full of cracks and holes may easily be covered with a coat or two of sand paint, a major weekend job ahead.

The sunlight draws me into a spacious back room. I take note; high ceilings, a non-working but attractive fireplace and then the light shining through two large windows.

I move closer to gaze upon top leaves and branches of a tall tree, one of many in the courtyard below. Reserved access for owners of elegant homes in the square below, me grateful for the view. I imagine mornings waking to the sunlight peeking through tree branches. I no longer care about the bathtub in the kitchen or the bathroom in the hall. My smile widens even further when I learn that the monthly rent is $125.00.

With new keys in hand I open the door to the realization that I am not alone in this space. I see and hear cockroaches scurrying across the floor. These non-paying residents, one of the inevitable realities of living in New York City. I leave the apartment confident of my first purchase, a roach bomb. Twenty-four hours after the bomb releases its poison, cautiously I open the door. The floors are covered with dead roaches. I hope I got them all... My new life in "the city" begins.

Walking home in the evenings I hear well known opera picks along with the aroma of broiling steaks as I pass by the Blue Mill's open windows. Warm memories of this old world Portuguese tavern, memories of sitting at the bar with the owner Arcino, watching the first televised viewing of Mikhail Baryshnikov performing a pas de deux from La Bayadere. Moving to New York to establish my own dance career, Arcino, an opera buff and balletomane, generously shares his enthusiasm with me. For the moment it is a perfect world.

IF ONLY

Demonizing one another fails us both. If I could come to understand the reasons for your admonishment. If only you might want to know the meaning for my withdrawal, could that help to bridge the gap between us? We are both mothers and daughters, living with the commitment to love justice and have mercy. For who are we who have not lashed out when feeling misunderstood? Who are we but ones who wish to be understood, forgiven and offered another chance to show our gratitude for our fortunes? Even when they sit next to our sorrows and misgivings.

I give up my hatred and resentment. Sadness is what lingers, knowing our shared histories, distinct in how we perceive them and troubled by our separate alliances. There were many times of shared understanding and mutual support, the most memorable for me being when my daughter was born and you generously shared your "Dr. Mom" love and advice. Earlier memories of us sneaking out after dinner, biking to the candy store where we filled our bellies with the sweetness we were unable to find at home. Shared losses when our beloved dog died, our grandparents passed, and the grieving disappointment when relationships failed, we held onto each other. These are the memories I choose. Deliberately, consciously letting the bitterness go. For what purpose does it serve except to inhibit breathing, tighten fists with arms crossed in anticipation of the next threat? I choose to keep my arms open and my lungs clear, ready to welcome the next embrace. And when keeping my arms open is difficult, I remind myself to slowly exhale and start again.

MY MOTHER'S EYES

My mother's eyes revealed so much, if she was feeling welcoming or rejecting, critical or delighted, focused or anxious. And when she was angry her eyes frightened me. There were other moments too when I watched. With a certain raised eyebrow in anticipation of a response, I could see her wandering eyes searching for recognition.

Her eyes black, always confused me as most eyes I knew showed a hue of color; hazel, and blue, green or brown. But my mother's eyes were midnight black, like a curtain shutting everything and everyone out. I remember the shift from smoky angry misery to a superficial show of pleasantry. The change in her eyes as she prepared a dish in the kitchen to the moment she entered the dining room to serve guests was like switching a TV channel from a scary mystery to an English drawing room drama. One expression among friends yielded to critical comment when she returned home. And when my father left her, an almost permanent glare of rage was impossible to escape. Her second husband brought back smiles and a gleam to her eyes. However, the bitterness never truly disappeared, a squint in the side creases revealing the pain of disappointment.

When my mother underwent cosmetic surgery, the pulled skin and lasered tone created a fixed appearance. It seemed as if her eyes were propped open. The surgery failed to produce the softness and tenderness one might want to see with an "enhancement." Now the tension looked immutable.

There were a few times when the softness in her eyes emerged. We would sit quietly together listening to a Brahms violin concerto or a Beethoven piano sonata. Her eyes closed; resting, releasing the strains of her heart.

DUST

hen I don't know what to do with myself I often begin to
clean. Sometimes it happens when I'm in the middle of a
thought or a sentence that has yet to find an end or when feeling
frustrated that the path, which seemed so clear and obvious, suddenly
results in a roadblock. A mental roadblock that kicked up all the
dust around me.

The light glares on filmy layers of gray blanketing wooden
slats on blinds. Green glass table lamp, books piled into bookshelves,
collecting at least a month's worth of gray powder . . . the effect of
human suffering revealed behind these closed doors. The need to
spray and wipe away worn out sorrows, mine as well as theirs, becomes
compelling. Bitter anguish so easily swept away with a clean soft
cloth. There is something so satisfying to be able to remove the
sadness, fear and loneliness . . . that entered this room.

Outside there is a breeze. I open the window for all
remaining gray to disperse, to welcome the next breath and light to
greet the next guest.

DREAM

There were times when I dreamt I was flying, floating over people below, simply spreading my arms to capture the lift in the next breeze. Weightless, passing through the trees catching the drift, flying felt natural, elegant, quiet. It wasn't for speed or travel. It was just the notion that I was no longer beholden to the ground.

In my dream I remember encouraging others to fly with me, telling them they might also be freed from the ground. These others were not distinct people in my life, not family or particular friends. They were just others, like myself, yet to realize they might also rise up into the air.

The wind fills the listless sails and suddenly the swishing of the hull cutting through the waves, the only sound as the dream resurfaces. Swimming too creates the buoyant, floating, weightless memory. Or when the ocean current sweeps my feet off its sandy floor.

WHY WE
write

AUTHORS TALK

JOAN CERNY

I have discovered that writing about one's life experiences is sometimes a more effective and satisfying way to process them than speaking endlessly about them. A different part of the brain is used when writing, so maybe it helps to exercise that part.

I feel so free in the writing group. One can write or say anything and not feel judged or censored. There is an interesting chemistry that develops in a group, which cannot be forced. It develops naturally, bringing many points of view together.

I so enjoy the gradual intimacy and knowing that grows with other group members who write about the core experiences of their lives.

EILEEN ERBECK

Writing is a form of healing. For all of us, in one way or another, isn't it?

Give me a prompt and the words just pour out of me—not all of them worthy to be seen by the outside world, but worthy of me. Recognizing the pain and joys of my life and being able to express them provides a richness that's soul-deep.

This intimate group of fellow-writers gives me a safe haven to bare my soul.

I've always been a writer of sorts, since childhood. But this is the first time I've allowed myself the luxury to have a regular writing practice.

I've come late to the joys of writing, singing, making art. They balance my decades-long career that I fell into, by chance.

NANCY GERBER

Through expressive, spontaneous writing—the kind we do in the
Write to Heal Group—we give birth to our selves. In the writing
group, our creative struggle is shared, witnessed, and validated
such that feelings of isolation and loneliness are diminished. The
ACAP Write to Heal group is a safe space where members challenge
themselves to reach deeply into their psychic reserve of memories,
thoughts, and feelings, composing this unconscious material into
vignettes, stories, and poems that move us with their deeply felt
emotions and stirring language.

ASHLEY GEROLSTEIN

Artist yes, but also a writer—a poet of sorts
Group experience encouraged *translucent*, free writes
Whatever came to my *scribbled* mind, not edited
Just in the raw, *shaded* thoughts being brought to new heights

Sharing evoked a broad *spectrum* of colors
Shades of *red* to keep private or to share
A group of eager *vibrant* ears to
Soothing *blending* emotions of listen and care

Response feedback in the *dark*, murky *brown*
Tormenting my *multicolored* mind
Fear of *fine green* judgment and concern
But faced with a *warm* face of kind

Returning to that journey of *gold* empowerment
To write about the *black and white fragments*
With shades of *gray* popping up
Visiting both my *smudged* past and somewhat *sharp* present

Extremely thankful and full of *mosaic* appreciation
For the opportunity to gather with *mixed media* others
Hope to engage in the delicate *rose* process again
Leading me to share my *paint-pen* confidently with another